# The Badass Is Back

KELLY DOHERTY KIMBERLIN

The Badass Is Back; How My Inner Badass Saved My Life

Publishing support by SJM Copywriting

# *The Badass is Back*
## How My Inner Badass Saved My Life

by Kelly Kimberlin

# Contents

# DEDICATION

I dedicate this second book to all the women in the world that may be going through hard times in their life. Life is not always easy and sometimes it can tend to be harder on the women, because we think we have to be Super-Woman all the time. Some of us have the habit of putting others before our own happiness and this can cause a lot of unnecessary stress. I am writing this book to let people know that life does not have to be so chaotic, so overwhelming, so damn stressful. When we connect to our own Inner Badass and do what we love, life can be filled with more joy, love, peace, and just plain happiness!

# FOREWORD

*Debbie Ketcherside*

H ave you ever felt so disconnected from your true self that you completely lost your own identity? You were so concerned about taking care of everyone else that YOUR dreams and goals really didn't matter anymore? Have you ever felt so low, that you started to wonder if this was all really worth it?

To me, my best friend had it all. She had two perfectly healthy daughters, an entrepreneurial husband that she was "able" to stay home and build a business with, a strong and outgoing personality and was always the life of the party. She could juggle it all and make it look easy. I have known her for over 30 years and she rarely complained. She knew how to handle everything that came her way.

Well at least that is what I thought...

In this book, you will find inspiration and guidance from someone who was able to pull themselves out of their darkest days of despair. Just when she thought her life wasn't worth living anymore, she was able to reach deep inside her soul and start taking the baby steps to become her true authentic self. This book is about not giving up and taking accountability for the choices that we make. It's about "Failing Forward", as the author states and just knowing those are life lessons. It's about believing in yourself but also being vulnerable enough to get help when you need it. Miracles happen every day when people start to do this.

Kelly is the perfect person to show you how this can happen. I remember after she became certified as a Life Coach and I heard her speak live for the first time. I literally sat there in awe. Who was this person and what happened to the Kelly I used to know? I could not believe how passionate she was about sharing her story and how much she had grown as a person. All of her hard work and self determination to fulfill her life's purpose had come full circle. She truly has found her passion in this world and can help you do the same. I urge you to take the time to connect with your inner badass and see how amazing it can feel!

# PROLOGUE

Years of being disconnected from my Inner Badass almost ended my life. After my father told me he wasn't wasting money on a girl to go to college I totally turned away from my authentic self. I knew I wanted to go away to college and get a degree in psychology, but when he said I should just get married, have kids and take care of my husband, that's what I did.

I actually set my dreams to the side and became a dental hygienist, because my brother thought that would be a good job for me. I just started doing what other people thought I should be doing and no longer followed my own inner voice, and this became the beginning of a very dangerous downward slide.

I got married young and started supporting my husband and all his dreams. And after doing that for so twenty-five years and denying my own desires I lost myself and got disconnected from my own inner power and that is when I almost ended my life. I was distracting myself from that inner urge I kept feeling about following my own dreams, which was to be a Life Coach. I had a *huge* desire to help people follow their dreams and to create a life that they love. Seems kind of ironic! It was such a strong feeling that it scared me, I wasn't used to doing what made me happy. I was way more comfortable making other people happy, so I kept ignoring those nudges.

But after twenty-five years, I ended up in my basement contemplating ways to end the pain that I was feeling deep inside. I no longer wanted to live like that. I felt dead inside, and I didn't think I could go on any longer. I didn't think it was possible to follow my own heart's desires, so I thought it would be easier to end my life. (That sentence is incredibly hard to write.) But then something happened. My little Inner Badass stepped in and said, "What the fuck are you doing? You are stronger than this! Now get your ass out of this basement and start saying YES to yourself!" So the Badass was back and she was ready to kick my ass into gear. This book will bring you through the journey of how I connected once again to my Inner Badass, so I could truly follow my Badass Soul's purpose and start living *my* life.

# CHAPTER 1

*Everyone Needs a Mama to Lean On*

T here I was in my basement, feeling sorry for myself, mentally drained and physically exhausted. I was tired of being tired! I felt alone, just like I did as a little girl, sad and lonely, spending a lot of time by myself. I had so much resentment built up for my husband Gary, blaming him for the condition I was in, blaming my parents for not being there for me emotionally, and blaming God for not helping me feel better. I was playing the victim game, playing a big martyr, something I learned well from my mother, God love her.

In my first book, *Street Wise and Alley Raised*, I really didn't talk about my real relationship with my mother. It is a hard subject for me to talk about. She was the most selfless, giving, kind woman that you would ever meet. Everyone loved her. But from the perspective of being her daughter, it had its ups and downs just like any other relationship. I know her lack of showing real love affected me. I knew she loved me, but I missed out on the affection, the hugs, the talks, the shit that I needed to help me through everything that went on in our house. Maybe I set the expectations too high for what a mother is supposed to be, but sometimes *I* felt like the mother, always getting in the middle of the fights and standing up for her. Because of that, I kind of lost my place. I was just a kid, trying to make everything around me OK, making sure my Mom was happy because she had a lot of stress in her life and I thought it was *my* job to take care of *her* and everyone else. She wasn't shown much affection from my Grandma either, so I think she just didn't know how. Her father died at forty-two years of age and my mother, being the oldest girl and middle child, took care of the house, made dinners and looked after her younger sister. I am sure she was done taking care of everyone by the time she had five children of her own.

My mom was a bit of a martyr, it wasn't easy living the life she lived with an alcoholic husband and five kids. She went from having a hard childhood to a hard marriage. So there she was doing everything again, taking care of the house, the kids, making all the meals and doing all the laundry and ironing. She even ironed handkerchiefs. I am pretty sure she was freaking tired of being tired herself. She felt sorry for herself and I understand why, and I'm sure I picked up some of those patterns from her. I worked full time and still did most of the household duties and all the kid duties and at the same time made sure everyone around me was happy. What I obviously learned was *I didn't deserve to be happy unless everyone around me was happy first.*

This is just one of the reasons that I took on so much and stressed myself out until I hit rock bottom. I was so disconnected from myself that I didn't know *who* I was, *what* I wanted, or if I was even *worthy* of more than just being a servant to everyone else's wishes.

As a teenager I was a little sassy with my mother at times, like most normal teenage girls are. I remember one time she was trying to correct me on something and I simply said, "Mom, I am seventeen, I know what I am doing." And if you are wondering, yes, the Karma from that incident has surfaced, and my own seventeen-year old daughter has already said that to me, plus many other things I probably said to my mother.

My relationship with my mother got a little distant, we didn't talk about much back then. She wasn't really into talking about important things, like a girl's menstrual period. Her definition of help was to give me a box of maxi pads and tell me to read what it said on the side. That was it. We also never talked about boys, sex drugs or alcohol. I am sure it was like this in many households at the time. She once said to me, "Don't tell me anything I really don't need to know." Like unless someone was bleeding or dying, she didn't want to be bothered. And we especially never talked about Dad being passed out on the kitchen floor and having to walk over him to get to breakfast.

I get it now, she had a lot on her plate and couldn't handle any more, especially teenage girl drama. I often thought having a sister to talk to might have been helpful. I just felt so alone most of the time, hiding out in my bedroom, trying to figure everything out by myself. My older brothers had each other and my younger brothers were close, and I was in the middle all alone. That is why I am so independent, and now it is extremely hard to ask for help. That's probably why I never reached out to my friends or family when I got depressed. I was so used to handling problems all alone, it just didn't feel normal to reach out. I mean, why would anyone want to help me?

I did ask my mom for help a couple times after I had kids, but that wasn't happening. She watched Maggie one time, only because I thought it would be fun for her to hang out with just her Grandma, her only grandparent left, as everyone else had passed away, even Gary's parents. But that was it, she said it was too much for her. I did ask her one more time when Maggie was five and had to get her tonsils out, I needed someone to watch Brooke. So, she did come over, but the surgery was delayed for a couple hours. It was my fault; I was so stressed and nervous about the surgery that I gave Maggie her vitamins, even knowing that she wasn't supposed to eat anything that morning. That meant they had to delay the surgery for a while so that the medicine wouldn't give her a bad reaction.

I asked Mom if she could still stick around to watch Brooke, and she continued to tell me she had a lunch date with her boyfriend, whom she saw almost daily, and couldn't stay. So I was going to have to take Maggie to the surgery center by myself so Gary could stay home with Brooke, all because my Mom couldn't do one simple little favor for me and *watch her own granddaughter!* I did not react to this very well. My Southside Badass came out and I said a few choice words and told her to get the hell out. I realized I couldn't depend on her, and I never, ever asked her for help of any kind again.

I know my mom had a rough life, and I know she deserved to have some fun her last years on earth, but that really hurt. It wasn't like we were going out to a party or having dinner out. My five year old was having surgery. Can you see why I am so freaking stubborn and independent? Like I get uncomfortable when people do things for me or try and give me things. I know deep down I'm expecting them to

I've mentioned an Inner Badass and now I'm letting you know about my Southside Badass. These are two different supportive characters within me, and within you too. Everyone has an Inner Badass, who helps direct them towards their own individual purpose and reason for life. For me, growing up the way I did, helped me create a Southside Badass, who helps me when things get especially tough, when I have to protect myself, when I have to stand up for myself. You may not have a Southside Badass, but you do have your own other Badass, who helps you out in specific situations.

disappoint me. This is another thing I have been working on all my life. I have had to learn how to receive.

All these things are clues to why I didn't feel important to anyone, that I wouldn't be missed, or that they all might be better off without me. Unfortunately this is where my mindset was at the time I was hitting rock bottom. Old patterns are hard to break, but I had to do something different if I was going to fix my life.

The main reason I am being so vulnerable and exposing how I grew up, how I felt along the way and what patterns I picked up as a child, is because I know I am not alone. I know there are other women from my generation that grew up in similar situations, or maybe even worse, and they feel the same way. I want to share my story so other women can start standing up for themselves too. Sometimes we try to convince ourselves that "This is just the way it is, this is the way I grew up, this is how my family is, depression runs in my family," whatever. But the truth is, *it doesn't have to be that way.*

Once we notice patterns and thoughts that no longer make us feel good, that no longer serve us, that is when we can change them. We can be different. We are not our parents, we are not our conditions, we have choices and we can make different decisions that work for ourselves and for our family. And this is what I had to start doing, to start making decisions that served my soul, served my dreams, served my purpose, because if I continued down the same "people pleasing" road I was going to die, slowly decaying from the inside out.

You know, most of us have some kind of parent issues. We can carry that through the rest of our lives and feel sorry for ourselves, or we can look at the situation with a different perspective. I am choosing to take the lessons I have learned from my life and change the pattern, to release the negative energy from my history, and maybe even laugh about it all.

I am refusing to let what happened to me in the past follow me through the rest of my life, and I feel so good about that.

Now I will sit and wait for my daughters to write their own book about how I fucked them up! Did I mention that Karma is a bitch?

*Two people-pleasing Mamas*

# CHAPTER 2

*Don't Be Afraid to Ask For Help*

I had to take control of my life. I had to learn how to make decisions that worked for me, that made me happy, that made me feel good, that made me feel worthy. I don't know where my self-esteem was, but it was never very good anyway. I had been working on myself for over twenty years and I still felt like shit. I had problems ever since I could remember, and I think that is what lead me to being bulimic at sixteen. I definitely think this was the beginning of the low self-esteem issues that carried way into my late forties. Being bulimic, which I never told anyone about except Gary until just a few years ago, was a very challenging time in my life.

The first time I admitted it to someone else, they actually had the audacity to say "OMG, I knew you had issues with food." And this was coming from someone that thought I was weird because I never fed my girls hotdogs for dinner. They could have them when we were out, but that was never a dinner item in my household. That kind of judgment scared me off from sharing with people, because I never knew how they would react. Being vulnerable to the wrong people can be dangerous, so be careful who you share your personal issues with. Not everyone is supportive and willing to help.

I had bulimia up until about twenty-three. I actually realized that if I didn't stop what I was doing, that I was going to destroy my insides and maybe even die. That was definitely a time in my life that I had to connect to my Inner Badass to save my life. I knew I could do it and I did. I have to give a little credit to my husband Gary, and you know I don't always like to do this, but he was probably the first person who ever really believed in me. He really helped me build up my self-esteem so I wouldn't do that to myself anymore. If you know me at all, Gary is the butt of most of my jokes, but he is really an incredible guy.

So, this is just to explain the state of mind I had throughout my life, why I felt the way I did. Not loving myself enough lead to self-abuse, which lead to bulimia. My life may have looked perfect to a lot of people, because I was taught not to talk about what was really happening in our household, so I had to fake it. God forbid people knew the truth. Isn't this the problem? Everyone thinks that the grass is greener on the other side, but over there they have the same fucking problems, or even worse! But no one is speaking the truth. I never want anyone to feel bad about their lives because they think mine is better than theirs. My life is not perfect, I am not perfect. You only see a little bit, so don't judge yourself because of what you see going on in my life. This is why I had to change the way I was living.

For some reason, God believes that I am strong enough for all these "fun" lessons. I keep telling Him thank you, and that I am done with learning, but He keeps sending them. I know now that I have this strong personality and this big deep voice for a reason, and I realized I had to start using it for good. I refused to have all my lessons just wasted. I decided I am going to use them to help others through all their bullshit. That's what got me out of the basement, knowing that I could make a difference in other people's lives.

As I was sitting down there, thinking of all the awful things I had gone through in my life, I actually got a very, *very* strong feeling that I had to help other women through their own shit and I was strong enough to do it. I was tired of hearing about so many women being on anti-depressants, women feeling inadequate, unfulfilled, and some even killing themselves. There was actually a woman in the neighborhood, I think she was only forty- two years old, who overdosed in the creek a block away from my house. I walk by that creek every day and I think about her and how alone she must have felt, how depressed she must have been to think about ending her life and actually go through with it, and I am determined to help as many women as I can to prevent them from getting to that point.

I was at that point in the basement, drinking to numb my feelings of depression and sadness. And when I started to look for the pain pills, because the alcohol wasn't, hoping maybe the pain would go away forever, I actually looked in the mirror and said, "What the Fuck are you doing? Is this it? Is this the example you want for your girls? They would not be better off without your, they need you! Gary needs you. Your Mom needs you. Your family would miss you, they *do* love you. Now get your ass out of the fucking basement and start making different decisions! Stop saying Yes to everyone but yourself. Find out what is wrong with you, get some help!"

I knew right then and there that the Badass was back.

# CHAPTER 3

*Reconnecting To My Inner Badass*

You know I often tell people I kept seeing my daughter's faces, when I got really depressed, especially Brooke because she was the youngest, and I wondered how they would survive without me. Here is a note she wrote me after I pulled myself back up. I read it when I need encouragement to keep going.

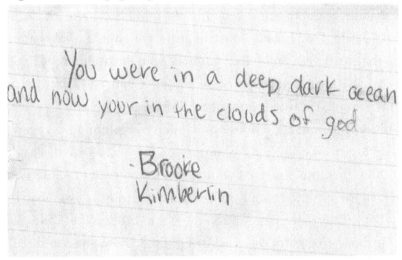

You were in a deep dark ocean and now your in the clouds of god

- Brooke
Kimberlin

But now, in some weird way, I think it may have also been my own little Kelly face, the little girl inside that was terrified of what was going on. It was the same lonely little Kelly that use to look out her bedroom window and wonder why her Dad wasn't coming home again that night.

She was scared. Who would take care of her and her family if something happened to him? They say that some emotions linger in your cells until you are ready to release them. Obviously those feelings never left. I could never console that little Kelly back then, I could never make things better for her, but I could take care of her now. She didn't have to be alone anymore. I was going to be there for her no matter what happened. I was going to help her stand up for herself this time. I was going to be there when she spoke her mind and I was going to help her stand up for all her dreams. That little Badass soul was ready to finally express herself just the way she wanted to and I wasn't going to ignore her anymore and I wasn't going to let anyone else ignore her either.

So, I got the hell out of the basement, put the alcohol away, and I decided to stop playing the victim, to stop being a martyr. I had this little soul that never got to been seen or heard and I had to be her biggest and best advocate. I was ready to make different choices that made *me* feel alive, that made *me* smile, that gave *me* some true inner joy. You know that joy, the kind you feel when you see a baby or a puppy and you instantly smile. I wanted more of that for *me* and my life.

This type of transition does not happen overnight. It has been helpful to keep a picture of little Kelly on my phone and at my desk to remind me of that precious soul that wanted to be loved, that wanted more out of life. Those reminders really helped on those tough days when I wanted to give up. That picture reminded me not to quit on that little girl inside me. I just had to get my sorry ass out of the way so she could really start living!

You see, when we come into this world, we are connected to our own Inner Badass soul. We know who we are and what we came to do. We are supposed to use our imagination and our intuition to grow and expand into the best versions of ourselves. We come into this physical form to have amazing experiences, incredible relationships, to travel, to invent things, to live full-out, but something happens to us and we forget how this was all supposed to work. It happens to most of us because we get conditioned by our families, peers, ministers, teachers, anyone with any kind of authority who thinks it is their job to tell us constantly what we should be doing and what we should be thinking. There are so many people passing along all their beliefs about everything in life that we actually stop thinking for ourselves and base all of our decisions on someone else's beliefs.

We don't know that is going on, but most of us are operating from whatever was passed on to us, like "That's just the way it is." The problem with this though, is that we get disconnected from ourselves and have no idea what we want to do with our lives. Ask any college student. Do you know 50% of kids enter college undecided and 33% of them change their major once they do decide? None of them are asking themselves what they would *love* to do. They are always looking outside themselves for the answers, but all the answers are within. We know this up until the age of five, but most of us get disconnected.

To get reconnected to ourselves, all we have to do is spend more time alone, without phones or TV, and ask ourselves questions about our life and how we want it to look. This is an inside-out job. More people need to look within themselves and then make the decisions based on what they themselves think and not give a damn about what others think. Right? You've heard the saying, other people's opinions of you are none of your business.

And this is exactly what happened to me. I knew at seventeen, I wanted to help people, I wanted to go into psychology, I was very interested in how people and their minds operated. But if you read the first book, you know my father didn't want me to go to a University. He insisted that I go to the Community college, because I was just a girl and he didn't want to waste money on me. He told me I was just going to get married, take care of my husband and have some kids, so I didn't need to further my education.

My Dad said he wouldn't pay for me to go to a University, but he never really said I couldn't go and pay for it myself. What if I had asked myself then, what I wanted to do? I might have done that, and my life might have turned out so differently.

It still confuses me that he insisted on straight A's in high school if he didn't want me to continue my education. Talk about some heavy conditioning going on at my house, but that is what happens to a lot of people, and we start believing what other people say about us. I certainly did. I took on that persona and became a wife and mother like he told me I would. But I wasn't truly happy. That is what can happen after years of not doing what you came into this world to do, and when people neglect what their gifts are, their lives become more stressful, chaotic, overwhelming and downright depressing because we are not following our soul's purpose. And when we don't use our gifts we not only miss out on being the best version of ourselves, but the world misses out too. It helps no one for any one of us to play small.

Why do you think so many people are on anti-depressants? There are so many people, especially women, who think they have to put themselves last before everyone else. Some people actually believe that they aren't worthy of anything better than what they have. People who think, Oh, I am not one of the lucky ones, I am not part of the wealthy club, I am not good enough to deserve great love, I am not smart enough to run my own business. All this conditioned, negative thinking is what almost took me out, and I knew that I was not alone, so I had to do something drastic.

I had to start saying "YES" *to myself!* Wow, what a concept. Am I allowed to do that as a woman? Will people still like me if I say "NO" to them? What will people think when I start doing what I want to do? What will they think when I just want to be with people who only make me feel good about myself? I knew I had to reconnect to my Inner Badass and say to hell with everyone else. I needed to do this to save my life.

*I am connected to my Inner Badass!*

# CHAPTER 4

*Being My Own Biggest Advocate*

S o where do you start when you are at rock bottom? You start slowly, you start making small decisions to get the ball rolling in the right direction. I knew if I made a lot of changes at one time, I would be right back where I started. The first thing I did was talk to Gary and explain to him my state of mind. Gary is really good at stepping out of the way when things get complicated, he just isn't much of a communicator about emotional stuff. He used to always tell the girls, just stay out of mommy's way when she starts getting crazy, and they did. He never really wanted to talk about it, I think it scared him too much. I think he saw it as approaching a mama bear trying to protect about 18 cubs! Could you imagine coming at me in the state of mind I was in, with a conversation about, "Hey, why are you acting so crazy?" Let's just say, it would not have been pretty.

I don't think he ever realized how bad it had gotten for me. He had no idea that I was done with living life as I knew it, and if we didn't change things I was going to walk away. It's funny how weird your thoughts get when you're depressed. I never imagined moving out and starting all over again with someone else, that sounded like way too much work. Instead, I fantasized about living in a one-bedroom apartment all alone, far, far away. Yep, that was my dream back then. I never pictured another man coming in on a white horse to take me away from all my craziness, because I knew I would just end up cleaning out the stables, washing his underwear and cooking for him! No thank you.

So, I explained to Gary that I did not want to be a landlord any longer, I wanted to sell all the houses, that I was tired of waking up in the middle of the night in cold sweats thinking we were going to lose everything. I also did not want to do anymore multi-level marketing businesses. I would still help him run our construction business, but that was it. I needed to take the stress out of my life and most of it came from doing whatever business opportunity Gary came across, I had to learn to say no to him. I had ideas of what I wanted to do and it was finally time to speak my truth. *Finally.* Wow, that felt so good, I never thought I would be able to say NO, I don't want to do that, I want to do this!

So what was that thing that I had been wanting to do for my entire life? To help others help themselves. I never really understood why most people's lives were so messed up, why everyone was so stressed, including myself. Was this the way life was supposed to be? I just thought there should be a way to make life more enjoyable. I was always counseling people to do and say what they truly wanted to. The funny thing is I never listened to my own advice. I was always telling people to stand up for themselves, to communicate their true desires with others, and how to truly love themselves, and there I stood not doing a damn thing to better my situation.

To be honest, I truly believe all this shit has been part of my journey. I had to go through all this chaos to be able to understand what other people would be feeling so that when I would be coaching them. I would be able to honestly look them in the eye and say, "I know how you feel." God must have known I was strong enough to handle what came at me in my life, and I am going to use if for good. I refuse to play the victim and feel sorry for myself any longer. I did that long enough.

I know some of you are reading this and thinking, *What?* Kelly always spoke her mind, so why didn't she speak up when it came to her own life? I just never saw it in the cards, I thought it was too late for me. I thought building a business with Gary was what I wanted. Anyone that knows Gary knows that he gets extremely excited about what he loves and I got wrapped up in his dream., I lost mine, so I just jumped right into his and thought that was what I wanted. Originally I wanted to go into psychology and my Dad talked me right out of that, so putting aside my dreams for someone else's is an old pattern that I had finally recognized and now it was time to change it.

So, forty-eight years into life I decided to stand in my truth and stand up for what I wanted to do. But the first thing I had to do was find out what was going on with my body. I couldn't sleep, it was like I had this energy surge at night, I was shaking all the time, my brain was foggy and I was extremely fatigue and edgey. I just felt CRAZY! I would lose my shit all the time for the dumbest things. For example:

One time I was driving my kids to school and a young girl threw her full soda and cup out her window on the street, right next to us. I just looked at her, shook my head and she sped off just to cut us off in traffic. Then we met up again in the parking lot of the high school and it was my turn to go in this long line and she cut in front of me with this grin that just set me off. I put that truck in park, started cursing up a storm like you wouldn't believe. Yes, I used the "c" word and I almost got out of the car, still in my pajamas, to take the bitch out. My kids were so embarrassed. They were saying things like, "Mom get in the car, Mom stop, Mom stop screaming!" I must have looked like a crazy bitch, but I didn't care. The attitude of this young girl just pissed me off and I lost it, and I didn't care how crazy I looked. I thought, *Who is raising kids like this,*

19

*that they think it is OK to throw their shit out the window, and drive like an idiot already at the age of 18?* UGH, I wanted to set her straight.

I tell that story to let you know just how fucking crazy I was at the time. Normal people don't do that kind of shit!

I know that whatever you put out into the world eventually comes back to you. It wasn't my place to straighten her out, the universe usually takes care of that. Karma came back to her eventually; she wrecked her truck later that year.

Then there was the time we were getting ready for Easter Mass and as usual, I was helping the girls get ready, picking out clothes, doing their hair and all of a sudden, I hear someone horning their horn outside. I asked the girls to look out the window to see who was honking, because I knew it couldn't be Gary, he knew better. They looked out the window, as I was trying to get myself ready, and when they turned their heads to look at me, I knew by the look on their faces that it was Gary. I said, "Tell me that is not Daddy honking his horn at us?" They nodded their heads yes, afraid to say anything else. I continued to get ready, thinking in my head, he must be nuts, thinking I would be OK with him honking his horn like that. All he has to do to get ready is take a shower, get himself dressed and jump in the car, maybe fifteen minutes tops. So, we go outside, get in the car, and by this time the Southside Badass is livid.

I got in the car and I said, "Why did you think it was ok to honk your horn at us?" He said he didn't want to be late. So we drove away and were a few blocks from home and I was lit up, done, *soooo* fucking tired of doing everything in the house. I did all the cooking, took care of the girls and the dog's needs, paid all the bills, did all the laundry, you name it, I did it, and he had the nerve to fucking *honk his horn* at me. So I told him to pull over so I could get the hell out of the car. As he did I was screaming at the top of my lungs, "Don't you ever even think about honking your horn at me again, EVER!" I turned to the girls in the back seat and said, "And don't you ever let a man fucking honk his horn at you!"

I also let him know he was not invited to the Easter lunch, and when they asked where Gary was, I simply said "He honked the horn at me this morning and will not be joining us." These are just a couple of examples of how on-edge and irritable I was all the time. And that's why I felt I had to go into the basement and hide out from my family, because I wasn't being a very nice person.. Going without sleep for months will affect your mood, and I knew I had to do something.

So, after I talked to Gary about selling all the properties and explaining the condition of my mindset it was time to find out why my body was not working. I made an appointment with my doctor's office and they did some blood tests and continued to tell me that everything was in the normal range and I just needed to get on an anti-depressant because I was hitting fifty. Any one want to guess what I had to say, in the state of mind I was in? I said, "Are you fucking kidding me? Is this what you are telling all the women that come in feeling like shit? This is all you can do for me? What the hell does *normal range* mean? DO you just think we are all just fucking crazy? You should be ashamed of yourself." I tore up the prescription they had given me and I never went back to that office ever again.

Now what? I knew I was not crazy, something was just wrong with my body. So, then I went to my hormonal specialist, that I had been going to for five years and she ran the blood work for all my hormones and thyroid like they do every 6 months, and she said they needed a little adjustment, but that wouldn't be causing all the issues I was having. I had already been getting testosterone pellets shot in my ass cheek every three months for six years (yes, women need testosterone too) already and had been on thyroid medicine since I had Maggie.

Sometimes I forget what my body has been through. For some strange reason I had no testosterone in my body. I found this out six years prior when I was going through another one of my "crazy times." I was so fatigued, exhausted and irritable all the time and I definitely didn't want anything to do with sex. I think I was only forty-one at the time. I knew I wasn't feeling good, but the doctors told me there was nothing wrong with me, that everything was in the normal ranges for my age. Listen up ladies, always get a second opinion and trust your gut if you think something is wrong with your body. You have to be your own biggest advocate. So once again I had to reach out to a specialist to get help. When the specialist checked and said my hormones were all in balance, I knew it was time for the next step.

Time for my "woo hoo" stuff. My energy ladies were the next stop for me. I believe there is a balance between energy work and medicine when it comes to health issues, that is why I went to the doctor first and then my energy healers. Now I just go to my energy people first when I have issues. Eventually I will have to look for another family practitioner, probably not a good idea to go back to the place where I threw a fit in the office.

So, I was in my very favorite chiropractor's office, Dr. Wendi Jones in St. Louis, and she has this gift where she can read the energy around your body. She can tell if you are having issues with your mind or your physical body, and then she is able to release whatever is causing your mental or health issues. So there I was lying on her table and she was running her hands up and down my body, moving her fingers around, and I was telling her I felt like shit and the doctor wasn't able to help me. She said, "Hmm, I can't get a reading on your adrenals."

I said, "What the hell are adrenals?"

She said, "Adrenals run your whole endocrine system and this is very serious, this is probably the cause of all your issues." Well I started sobbing like a baby. Finally, someone had validated that I was not crazy, that something was wrong with my body. It felt like a ton of bricks just left my shoulders. I knew right then and there I was going to get better, because knowing what the issue was would be the key to my healing.

She continued to tell me how serious this is because my adrenals were not functioning at all. That would explain why I felt so bad. She explained that extreme stress causes adrenal fatigue, and that I had to get the stress out of my life if I wanted to start feeling better. "Yeah right," I said, "How in the hell am I going to do that?"

She looked me right in the eye and said, "Your life depends on it. This is nothing to mess around with." Usually Wendi is pretty laid back and not so serious, so I knew she meant what she said, so I had to start thinking of ways to destress my lifestyle.

She also told me to start doing breath work, meditation, along with some yoga and to schedule several appointments with her. And, most importantly, to remember I was not going to get better overnight. I was ok with that, I was just so freaking happy that I continued to cry as she was talking.

Then she pulled out the big guns. She started with acupuncture; I had so many needles in me it wasn't funny. Then she pulled out her crystals, magnets and her magic infrared light and I felt better instantly. I am pretty sure part of feeling better was due to the fact that I had a diagnosis and was ready to do whatever it took to heal. I truly believe that she saved my life. I could not have gone on much longer feeling the way I was feeling. I continue to see Wendi several times a year just to keep my energy and health as balanced as I can.

So I went to Wendi for about 5 or 6 appointments that year and started doing yoga right away. I also started putting greens in my shakes because that was supposed to help also. You can imagine all the Google searches I did for adrenal fatigue. I learned all kinds of things and I was willing to try anything to repair my damaged adrenals. I can't explain how good it felt to be on the road to recovery. It was truly life changing.

When your adrenals are under stress, they release adrenalin and cortisol hormones, like you are in a "flight or fight" situation all the time, not just during stress. I guess I was lucky that I didn't kill anyone. And this also explains why my hands would be shaking and why I couldn't sleep, why I would actually be wide awake at night, feeling like a bear was going to attack me at any moment and I had to be ready.

That's why yoga was really good for me also. I did that about four times a week and it changed my whole body, I could feel myself getting calmer and I was in amazing shape. I also started doing meditation, not perfectly, but I continue to do it every day because it helps keep me centered and calm, and that too has changed my life. But my very favorite de-stressor is getting outside, especially when I have time to go hiking deep in the woods.

There is something that happens to me when I am in nature. I immediately get relaxed and calm, and it truly helps me feel better. I could tell all the new things I was starting to do were working for me because I had not attacked any young stupid girls since then. So the biggest lesson I have learned through all of his is that you have to be your own biggest advocate. If you feel like something is wrong with you and your doctors just want to keep medicating you, go get a second or third opinion! We are not meant to live life all drugged up. It is good sometimes for short terms and special circumstances, but I believe more and more people are given prescriptions for the wrong reasons.

# CHAPTER 5

*Taking Time To Heal*

T hat was just the beginning of the physical healing process. Believe me, it has been a long one and it is something I continue to keep up with as maintenance for my body. I recently met a Functional Medicine doctor here in St. Louis, Dr. Seth Gerlach, who has helped me tremendously. I really messed up my digestive system, stomach and liver along the way and he was able to get everything back in balance and I continue to work with him on a regular basis. I love working with Seth because he focuses on the core issues that are causing the problems, not the symptoms. Because if you just treat the systems, the core issues never go away and people just keep taking medications to cover up the real problems, and this becomes a vicious cycle.

Looking back, taking care of my health issues might have been the easy part compared to what I was in for next, but I was willing to take those next steps to help me move forward in my life. The real inner work was about to begin. God help me. While learning how to take care of my body I also knew I had to take care of my mind, my soul, and my little Kelly. I had neglected these things so long because I had been in survival mode and didn't understand that these things might have been as important or even more important than my health issues. I also learned that my mindset had probably been a factor in my health issues. I had so much anger and resentment built up in my body that it really messed with my mind, which in turn, affected my health.

So, I went searching for a coaching program, I knew after reading hundreds of books about how we create our own lives and how this whole universe thing works, I wanted to learn more so I could help others. I had been very curious about how we are all operating and living in this world, and I had read books by Deepak Chopra, Eckhardt Tolle, MaryAnn Williamson, Wayne Dyer, Louis Hay, anyone I thought I could learn something different from. I knew I wanted a coaching program that was more spiritual-based and I was ready to find the perfect one for me. Even more than that, I had to find a spiritual community.

I had been raised in a strict Irish Catholic family and assumed all the beliefs of my family, but it never felt right to me. I was more interested in my spirituality than my religion, but we weren't taught very much about spirituality. It was more about the dogma of the Catholic religion and what you could and could not do if you wanted to get to Heaven. Well, by the time I was 16, I thought, *Oh well, I'm fucked, what is the point of even trying anymore, I have broken half the commandments already!* Hell, I almost even broke "Thou shalt not kill." I got very curious about other religions especially after I had kids of my own and I wasn't sure I wanted to raise them in the Catholic church. I didn't think it was too safe to say anything or try anything different while living under my father's roof. "My house, my rules!" he would always say. So now it was time to try something new.

In order to find a community, Gary and I checked out all the different churches in our neighborhood to see if they felt any different or better than the Catholic church. We tried several Lutheran churches, a Baptist church, a couple non-denominational, a Methodist and I think at one point we even joined a cult. We discovered we were in a cult when they tried to occupy all of our time so no one could tell us how crazy they really were. I remember our last day there, they wanted to meet and have a bible study on the day of the St. Patrick's Day parade, my birthday!! Those people were crazy, I was just glad my Southside Badass kept her cool. We were just getting so uncomfortable with them telling us what we should be doing with my time, and that is when we decided to leave that church and never answered their calls again.

Gary and I laugh so hard when we think about all the times we were baptized! Every church wanted to baptize us in their religion, because they thought *they* were only ones with the right way to do religion. One church even tried to baptize Gary in the river, late one night, with a bunch of men, but he didn't want any part of that. So they ended up using a big walk in pool because that particular church believed in full immersion. Just one of many.

We sometimes sit around have a glass of wine and reminisce about all the crazy things we have gotten ourselves into, because that shit is funny. Humor gets you through a lot of stuff in your life. I guess we were so desperate to find a spiritual community where we could raise our family we were willing to try anything. Finally, after years of searching, we landed in a spiritual-based community that really works for us.

I hope everyone out there is feeling a little better about their own life after hearing about the Kimberlin shit show. The Kardashians have nothing on the Kimberlins. You're welcome.

Anyway, back to the coaching. While Gary and I were getting baptized left and right, I needed coaching help. I started looking at programs that would help me grow, so I could eventually help others. I think I looked at about four or five different coaching programs, and when I say Mary Morrissey from the Life Mastery Institute, I knew immediately this was perfect for me. I knew that it had everything in it that could help me get through this tough time in my life and I loved how the coaching program was set up for me to transform my life. Now, it wasn't cheap by any means. It was over $10,000 to get all the first program's material and to go out to Los Angeles to get certified, but I was all in and Gary supported me along the way. It's a funny thing how the universe takes care of you when you step towards your dream. I put that $10,000 on a credit card and just knew it would work out, I learned this principle from the books I had been reading, and two months later I was gifted almost that exact amount of money. I just knew that I was taking the right step in the right direction to fulfill my dream of becoming a life coach.

The first person I had to coach on these new principles and life skills was myself. I had to do this, or else I was going to be miserable the rest of my life. Living according to other people's beliefs for almost forty-eight years had not worked for me. I jumped right in, I consumed every aspect of those audios and workbooks as fast as I could. And a funny thing happened – I could actually *feel* my body changing, I was getting goose bumps every time I read something or heard something I knew was especially for me. I fell in love with the Dream Builder program and I couldn't wait to go to training.

There was a lot to do before I headed out to Los Angeles to get certified. I went through the training online at least four to five times which lead me through some really big life-changing practices that I had to implement in my life. I had completely denied my soul's purpose most of my life and I had to reconnect to it. I had awful self-esteem, so bad that I actually hated myself for getting so depressed. And I also had a lot of resentment issues to deal with. I had to learn how to forgive myself and others, and I also had to find my worthiness by just being me. Then, for the first time in my life, I had to start thinking about what I wanted my own career to look like. Shit, there was a lot of work ahead of me.

Working on uncovering some of the deep-rooted emotional stuff that was causing me to not feel worthy was extremely hard. I had to go through and actually release those emotional blocks so I could start moving forward in my life towards the things that mattered to me. I learned that unforgiveness, resentment, and anger are constrictive energies that will stop you from growing and evolving into what you truly desire. There was a lot of journaling, crying, screaming, thinking, and actually a lot of quiet time with just myself. This was all new to me, I was used to just moving through things, not thinking or talking about them, but those were just old patterns and habits that I had to work on. I had to be aware of what I was thinking about myself and my life and I had to rethink, repattern and start fresh. Not so easy at forty-nine!

It was a major shift for me to start thinking for myself, to actually say, "Are these thoughts helping me grow or keeping me stagnant? Are these emotions constrictive or free flowing? Are these thoughts going to help me love myself so I can grow, or are they going to make me feel bad about myself?" I have learned over the years that we all have to be more aware of what we say and how we feel. Awareness is key.

I have to say, this has been one of the hardest things I have ever been through, I would feel like I was doing better and then I would fall right back into self-hate again. Or I would think I was strong enough to help someone, and then fear, doubt, and worry would set in and slow me down. Talk about a roller coaster, I almost gave up many, many times, but then I would remind myself that I was trying to change thoughts and patterns that I had lived with for almost forty years. It does not happen overnight. I can tell you this, two years in and I feel so different, so calm, way more at peace, and the Southside Badass rarely has to show up any more. But I know I am different, I am able to let go of the old me, the old story and start living from my true authentic self

It is like a rebirth of myself. I always say, there is more Kelly coming out every day. I am actually getting to know who I really am and what I truly desire by looking within, asking my heart and not my head. I am loving myself enough to give myself time to heal, time to discover the real me and she is pretty cool.

I could not have said that 2 years ago.

# CHAPTER 6

*Time To Breathe Again*

T here was another thing that I had to deal with that I was putting off for years. I couldn't breathe through my nose because of a deviated septum that I had since birth. Yes, since birth. My Mom and Dad claim that I was born with a broken nose. They think it happened when my Mom fell while she was pregnant with me. I have been told I wasn't the cutest baby ever: I was jaundiced, had half a set of black hair, and a broken nose. That doesn't sound too cute I guess. Maybe that is why there are very few pictures of me, even though I was the only girl out of five siblings.

So, I have always had trouble breathing through my nose and it was worse at night. I had rhinoplasty surgery when I was about nineteen, but it didn't turn out so good. I remember that surgery like it was yesterday. I was in the surgery center on the operating table and the nurse came in to get the IV started, but she couldn't find a good vein. Now, at fifty-two years old, they would have a huge variety to choose from, but at nineteen not so much. So she had two other nurses come in to try. *Try*, like I was a guinea pig, they couldn't get one started either no matter how many times they poked me. I was dying, it hurt so bad, I looked at them and said, "Get away from me and get a freaking nurse in here that knows what the hell she is doing." Finally, about forty minutes later the last nurse got the IV in one try. But that was just the beginning of the surgery from hell.

Taking that long to get the IV started wasn't a big deal because the doctor was running about an hour late anyway. I remember him running in, with his cowboy boots on, rushing around the room, and then just shoving some cocaine in my nose. Yes, that is not a typo: cocaine. Supposedly that is what they did back in the day to numb your nose, they didn't bother with general anesthesia. This guy was moving so fast, not even taking the time to explain anything, I was thinking to myself he might have had a quick sniff himself.

I don't know where that guy had to go, but he was in such a hurry he didn't even bother to give the cocaine time to go into effect before what was coming up next. Seven shots to my nose. I was not prepared for pain like this and I was screaming at the top of my lungs, "STOP, I can feel that!" But he just ignored me and claimed the cocaine should be in affect already. If you've ever been punched in the nose several times in a row, you have an idea what it felt like. It was horrific. Good thing I was tied down, because I was actually trying to get off the table. I wanted to get the fuck out of there. I was livid, between the IV shit show and now this, I thought my parents had brought me to some fucking whack job that didn't know what he was doing.

About five minutes later the cocaine finally set in and I was higher than a kite. I started to get calm and a little silly, and I wanted them to move the mirror on the ceiling so I could watch. WTF, watch? I *must* have been high. So, he took this big-ass plier-looking thing and BROKE MY NOSE to reset it, and I could actually hear it crack. It was probably one of the worst experiences of my life. They finally finished up, put a brace on my nose and sent me home. I was miserable for several days. It was so painful because of the break and then I find out there were 3-inch tubes up my nose causing all kinds of discomfort. I only found this out when we called the doctor's office because I was in such pain, and they told my Mom that I could take out the tubes. Oh my God, it was like pulling out that long ass handkerchief thing that clowns pull out of their sleeves, you know, the one that never ends, it just kept coming and coming. The pain instantly went away. Knowing him, he probably put the wrong ones in, or maybe he did it on purpose because I was such a shit.

We went back a week or so later for them to check on the progress and I still wasn't breathing easily. He must not have done a very good job.

Guess what? They wanted to do it again. Well, you probably know what my answer was to that: "*Oh hell no!*" I thought, *Never ever again will I have nose surgery, I could live forever without breathing through my nose.*

Thirty years later, I still couldn't breathe through my nose, and I began thinking this might be causing the sleeping issues I was having. So I got an opinion from a different doctor that a good friend referred me to, to check out how they were doing rhinoplasty thirty years later. Well this new doctor had me at, "general anesthesia". I signed up right away. I was tired of not being able to breathe out of my nose.

Gary brought me to the surgery center about a month later, and as I was going in, I told him I should be out in a couple hours. Five hours later they were wheeling me out of surgery. It took that long to fix my deviated septum. I often wonder if that first doctor made it worse. I know his surgery didn't take five hours. The plastic surgeon did a great job, I can now breathe through my nose and sleep better at night. He could have fixed the little bump on the bridge of my nose while he was in there, but he didn't. He claims that was cosmetic. I don't have a perfect nose, but that keeps my imperfections in the forefront to remind me I don't have to be perfect to be happy.

As you can see, I was trying anything and everything to repair my health and my state of mind. The first couple years were tough. It was not easy working on changing my patterns and habits that weren't good for me anymore. And changing my people-pleasing behavior has been the toughest challenge of all. It was so instilled in my mind that making other people happy gave me self-worth. That other people's happiness had to come before my own. I still have to stop myself occasionally from checking in with others before I check in with myself.

I still had a lot of mornings that I wanted to give up, mornings where I would open my eyes and say," *Fuck*, why do I still feel like shit when I am working so hard on getting better?" I really had a hard time with this part. I thought since I knew what my issues were (but you never really know what they all are at one time) that I would do all the right things and everything would be OK. It wasn't, but at least this time I didn't give up, instead I just kept going in the right direction. I kept taking baby steps that felt good so I wouldn't get overwhelmed with all the changes I had to make. Step after step got me some momentum in my life, and I now felt empowered to do more for myself.

I also work hard on not playing a victim anymore. My Inner Badass won't let me. I have learned over the years that when you own your successes and your mistakes, that life can be challenging and rewarding at the same time. Owning that I created the hot mess in my own life empowered me to know that I could then create something even bigger and better. I just kept taking small steps in the direction I wanted to go in, not the direction I thought others wanted me to go in. I have learned the lesson that following what others think you should be doing does not necessarily work out all the time, and sometimes it can even be detrimental.

# CHAPTER 7

*The Best Medicines*

I n between all the inner and outer healing I was working on, I also started to reach out to my girlfriends a lot more. When I was depressed I tended to keep to myself. Between not feeling good and being embarrassed about not having it all together, I didn't want to be around anyone. This is probably the worst thing a person could do when they are down and out. I knew I was super focused on feeling sad and I knew I had a long road ahead of me, but I also knew if I didn't start hanging out with my girlfriends more it would be harder. `

I don't know about other women, but I think hanging out with girlfriends that make you laugh until you pee yourself, women that don't judge you, and women who love you just the way you are is one of the best medicines you can have. I am extremely lucky to have these types of girlfriends in my life, so I started reaching out.

Now I didn't really start going into my story when we got together. I was tired of my story and I just wanted to laugh, like serious belly laughing, and that is what always happens. I have been known for laughing so hard that I have to squat to prevent peeing myself. For example, I was up in Chicago with my high school friends Marcia, Marge, Theresa, and Teresa. We were there for a weekend to visit our other friend Stathy, and we were out at a bar. Now sometimes when we are out we like to smoke cigarettes when we are drinking, maybe we think it makes us look cool or sexy, I am not sure. So we were drinking and smoking and Marcia starts looking down at the floor like she lost something. I said, "What are you looking for Marcia?" She said she lost her cigarette, then all of a sudden, she looked down at her boobs and there it was, in between her breasts. She nonchalantly took it out of her shirt and started smoking it again like it was no big deal. Well I laughed so hard, I was down in a squat for at least five minutes. Silly shit just cracks me up and I needed a lot of that.

There have also been many weekend trips with my other girlfriends, Deb, Stathy, Yvette, Tammy, Sue, and Sandy. We either fly or drive to somewhere new and from the moment we get in the car to the moment I drop them all off at home, we are laughing. There is something about just getting away with your favorite people, and the fact that you don't have to take care of anyone besides yourself is so relaxing. We stop when we want, eat when and whatever we want, stay up until all hours of the night, and get up when we damn well please!

I also spent many a night at my girlfriend Debbie's house with several of my other friends. She is single and is always having us over for girl time. We either go out to dinner, try and find some good music somewhere or go to a concert, and then head back to her house and cap the night off with a bottle of wine and talk till we pass out. We have had so many laughs late night in her family room or out by the pool, and that has been a life saver. I know laughing can actually change the energy in your body and I could feel it, so I am back to regularly reaching out to friends.

Music is another thing that helps me heal. I have been using music to elevate my mood for years. When things were a little difficult in my house growing up, I would head up into my brothers' room, in the attic, put their big head phones on and listen to all their albums. The good stuff, like Stevie Wonder, Foreigner, Bee Gees, Donna Summer, KC and the Sunshine Band, Earth Wind & Fire, and the Doobie Brothers. I would be up there for hours and it was a life saver. I still do that sometimes. Not the attic, but the music. When I am in a funk, I turn up my music nice and loud and dance around like crazy. I also try and have music playing whenever I can, it really shifts my mood.

Walking can also change a mood. I work out of my house a lot and always start my day walking the dogs. Even when it is cold, I bundle up and just walk around the block to refresh myself. Sometimes in the middle of the day if I have been in the house too long, or I feel like I need to move my body, or the dogs are glaring at me for another walk, I get up and walk again. Moving your body moves your energy and that is good, especially when you are stuck in a problem and can't seem to find an answer. Sometimes it helps to ask a question before I take my walk, like, "What would be the best way to help this client?", or "Should I charge more for my services?" Then I just walk and I don't overthink it. And when I come back I feel like I have the right answer.

And my very favorite thing to do, to help me release any negative energy trying to pull me down, is getting a massage. I know shitty energy can get stuck in your body and cause a lot of health issues, because I have lived it. So, keeping up with things like massages really helps me keep up with my health. Like I said earlier, I do not want to go backwards and end up in the rabbit hole again, so I insist on doing things that make me feel good and help me maintain a healthy lifestyle.

Finding out what helps you feel good is important to get through this thing called life. We all have enough stress in our lives, enough have to's, enough should have's, but we need to do more things that we *want to do!* Life is not about doing what others think we should be doing or what society thinks we should be doing. It is about living a life that lights us up. We are supposed to be checking in with ourselves to see if we would love it, not check in with everyone else to see if it is right for them. Do more of what turns you on, hang out with people who make you laugh, and yes, dance around like no one is watching, and see how you start feeling. This is when things started to change for me and I want everyone to have this feeling. A feeling of, "Yes I love my life, yes I love myself, and I am OK just the way I am!"

# CHAPTER 8

*Badass Self-Esteem*

W hat self-esteem? I never really had any, I had been faking it for years. I never really thought I was good enough for anything of my own. I never thought I was good at anything important. Growing up with brothers that were three and seven years older than me never gave me any confidence, there was no reason to compete with them on anything. They were super smart, always got straight A's and got scholarships to college. Well, that wasn't happening for me, an A/B student. They also played a lot of sports and of course were very good at that too. I can tell you I never got player of the game at any of my sports events. I thought I was good at volleyball, but didn't make the high school team, only the softball team and they put me out in right field. I remember being so nervous playing, I don't even know why I was out there. I think I assumed I had to play a sport because that is all my brothers talked about. I didn't even care that my dad never came to a game, because he would have pointed out all the mistakes I had made, and I made a lot!

I am not writing this to have people feel sorry for me, these are just the facts to explain why I had such low self-esteem. Hell, three of my brothers are doctors and the other one owns his own business. I know I am not a dumb bunny. Like my father said, "Kel, you may not be as smart as your brothers, but you are street wise and alley raised." It's funny, and it's true. I am not book smart like my brothers, but I have a lot of wisdom and common sense that has gotten me through many tough times, and I think that is what I needed to make it this far and why it is good for me to use those gifts to help others through their tough times. I am using my gifts for good. I finally reached a point in my life that I get it, I get that we are all different and we should all be using our amazing gifts to help ourselves and to help others.

So, working on my self-esteem has been fun! I don't know if you know about mirror work, but I had to do a shit-ton of it. I actually had to look in the mirror every morning and say "I love you" to myself, over and over again, and it was weird, I could barely do it. That was a lot of work. I realized, while doing mirror work, that I hardly ever looked myself in the eyes. *Wow.* Even when I did make-up, I would look at my face and outline of eyes, but very rarely right into my eyes. That's bizarre right? It makes me sad that I had gotten to the point where I couldn't even look at myself, I actually hated myself that much that I disgusted myself.

But I kept doing the mirror work because after going though all my training, I finally understood how important it is to truly love yourself and that you cannot love anyone else before you can love yourself first. Mirror work can actually help you start feeling more empowered and confident to do the things you truly want to do. And to be honest, I was exhausted from putting myself down all the time, I am sure there are plenty of other people doing that for me.

I continued to tell myself things that no one ever told me, like, you are wise, you are smart, you are giving and caring, you are loving, you are funny and you are *deserving*. Yep, deserving of a great life, deserving of great love. Still the feelings of self-hate and self-doubt would come back on a regular basis, and I had to start being aware of those constrictive thoughts and change them every time to something empowering. Now I can say I love myself, I am worthy of all good things and actually believe it. And when the self-doubt tries to creep in at this point in my life, I can release it a lot faster than before, because I am so much more aware of how this actually slows my progress down.

That mirror work really helped me to see the actual little girl inside of me, the scared little Kelly that didn't understand why she didn't feel loved, by herself or by others. I continue to look at her on a daily basis to make sure she knows that it is OK, that she doesn't have to be afraid anymore. This changed everything for me, but it took time, a long time, but it was worth all the work. I invite you to do the same thing, see how it makes you feel, see if you can do it and really mean what you say. It is crazy how you can actually feel your energy change, you start to feel lighter, calmer, more at peace. You eventually might even be able to do it with a shitty little grin on your face, saying HELL YEAH, I am amazing!

I also had to learn how to change the language within my bitchy monkey mind that was going 24 hours a day. I was one of the worst self-talkers ever. I would get so mad at myself for everything: when I would forget somebody's name at a function, or if I would not spend enough time with the kids, if I would work too much or not enough, if I would cut someone off when they were talking. Anything that I did wrong, I just thought I was an awful human being. But here is the thing, I am a human being and I am not perfect. Actually, I believe I am a spiritual being having a human experience, but the point is, I am not perfect, and I don't have to beat myself up for every little thing that I "think" I am doing wrong. The judging of myself and others had to stop. I have learned over the years that it isn't serving anyone being so judgy.

I also started practicing affirmations on how I wanted to be and whom I wanted to be. Just like the mirror work, I would do my *I am* statements to create the person that I desired to be. *I am* kind, *I am* patient, *I am* a successful coach, speaker and author, *I am* helping people help themselves, and *I am* an example of self-love. Watching what you say after an *I am* statement is extremely important, because you are co-Creating with your God, with your Universe all the time. Be aware of how you talk to yourself and about yourself, and watch how you start changing the language when you become more aware of the damage you could be causing yourself.

I choose to continue this work on a daily basis because I know it has helped me move in the direction that I want to take in my life. I can only imagine what other people thought when I announced that I was going to be a life coach. OMG, I can hear the laughter now, because it is way out of the box for the people who knew me. But I always knew deep down that I was different, I didn't know why, but I didn't want to do what everyone else was doing. I just don't understand why people do things just because they think it's the right or only way to live life.

I got married very young, which no one was doing, because they were still in college. I didn't have kids for twelve years because I wasn't sure that was what I wanted to do, while everyone else had kids right away. We moved into the city, not too many people were doing that, a lot of them went out west as far as they could. Gary and I both quit our jobs to own our own business, not always a smart thing to do or an easy thing to do. We bought a lot of houses and rehabbed them before it was a popular thing to do. Gary and I have failed in a lot of different things and we can tell you what doesn't work, but I know we are in the game, we are getting up to bat and will continue every day.

All of this is doing what we wanted to do, not just what everyone else expected. Yeah we failed, but I call it failing forward. Getting certified to be a life coach probably made people question my decision. Like, "what is she doing now?" Who does she think she is?" "How could she help anyone when she is a hot mess herself?" "She is never going to make money doing that" "That will never last." In order to ignore what other people have said, or might have said, I have to have a strong sense of self and know that I know what I am doing. I have to continually empower and encourage myself with positive self-talk to build up my self-esteem, and I also have to be aware of what I am saying about myself in order to help me move forward with my business.

I also do a lot of the things that make me happy, that keep me centered. Like I said before being out in nature, especially in the woods, changes me, I can actually feel my energy changing out there, so I get outside as much as possible. If I can't get into the woods I actually just go outside and get my bare feet on the grass, on the ground and I visualize myself connected to the source of the earth and that keeps me grounded. I also start my day listening to guided meditation, for 30 minutes before anyone else gets up, this keeps me extremely grounded and calm. If I have an extremely busy day I simply just stop what I am doing and sit in silence for a few minutes, to simply re-charge so I can handle the rest of the day. And of course, I breathe, where I am aware of my breath and I am breathing all the way from my belly: in for a count of six, holding for three, out for six, holding for three. This calms me. Some of us actually don't realized that we aren't breathing at times of stress, so being aware and doing in purposely is important. Try it yourself.

I think one of the many challenges in life is to keep your confidence high about the decisions you have to make, and not give a fuck about what people think! I mean it, you can take all their advice, listen to people you might think have your best interest at heart and then sit with yourself and *you decide* what is best for you. Isn't this what we tell our kids? At least, I do! I tell them to listen in school and pay attention to what lights them up inside, do their best and do what they think is best for themselves. Yes, they will all make mistakes, but that's how this all works. Encouraging them to follow their hearts and connect to their own Inner Badass will serve them well.

We all should be following our own intuition more, and do what we think is best for us and the people around us. The mistakes and failures are necessary for learning the lessons we need to learn to expand into the best versions of ourselves. And I can guarantee, learning from your own mistakes and not from other people's ideas will be so much better in the long run.

We have to make mistakes, that is the only way we can grow into something new, something bigger and better. We came into this world to have experiences and to expand and grow into the true authentic beings we were meant to be. If we don't, life just stays stagnant and stressful, we tend to get overwhelmed and depressed about our lives and it doesn't have to be that way. I know a lot of people are afraid of getting out of their comfort zone. It can be really scary, but the rewards are worth it. They say the most successful people in life are not comfortable unless they are uncomfortable, because it means they are moving into the bigger versions of themselves and it keeps them motivated.

We don't just want to wait for everything to come to an end. Let me tell you, its way more fun out of the comfort zone. You could die of boredom in there! Been there, done that, now it's time to live life to the fullest. I not only do this for myself but as an example for my girls. They have seen me at my lowest, which really affected me at the time. I felt extremely guilty about them seeing me like that. But they also saw me pull myself out of it and they saw me getting stronger and stronger as I went through all the struggles, and that makes me feel amazing. I now know that they understand that people fail and fall down, but they also know they can make it through anything if they connect to their own Inner Badass.

I continue to share my failures with my daughters because they need to know that it is OK to fail and get back up over and over again and to not get distressed over it, it is the way of life. I talk about my struggles and what lessons I have learned from them so they understand life does not have to be perfect for them to be happy. And I have also taught them that laughter can get you through anything. I laugh at myself all the time because some of the shit I have been through is unbelievable and so laughable.

It's so funny that some people think being perfect is the only way to live. I believe trying to be perfect just adds more stress to your life. My father use to say, "Don't try and be so perfect, nobody is perfect." And he was absolutely right, perfection takes a lot of work and it also takes a lot of the fun out of life and I am no longer interested in that.

So, to this day my Inner Badass insists that I have a daily practice of loving myself and all my imperfections. I also have learned how to forgive myself on a daily basis, and to center myself and to keep myself grounded consistently. I now truly see myself as worthy of anything I desire in my life, as long as I am not harming others in the process. Why do I continue to do all these things? Because while having low self-esteem and no confidence can prevent you from living a life that you love, the opposite is exactly true too. And I am living proof of that.

*I am a worthy Badass!*

# CHAPTER 9

*The Distraction Game*

A nother thing I had to work on was distraction, which is the avoidance of things that were truly going on in my life. I totally neglected how I was truly feeling deep down inside. I think it terrified me to actually think about it. Let's see, what were my favorite distractions? Being super busy was my favorite. I kept my calendar pretty full so I could avoid really sitting with myself and seeing what was missing, seeing why I was so miserable inside. And I loved when people asked me what I was up too, oh boy, could I go on and on with all the stuff I had to do. It was almost like I was trying to validate my worthiness, my place in this life. Now I was pretty busy but I know I could have put some time aside to take care of myself, and maybe then I would not have ended up in the basement hiding from my family.

Another favorite distraction was being on my phone. I was a bit of a Facebook whore, I wanted to make sure no one was having more fun than me. I also loved to watch a lot of TV at night, a lot of reality TV, which I still do, but I usually fall asleep after 30 minutes. Shopping was also a way to numb any emotions and of course drinking earlier and earlier in my day to numb the buzzing and to numb my emotions. I am sure I have more, and I tend to do some of these things occasionally, but I think that is OK, as long as it doesn't become a habit so strong you no longer feel what you need to feel.

Some of you might think, *What is so bad about numbing your emotions? I don't have time to feel my emotions, I don't want to think about what has happened, I want to move on.* Well, that is what I did and look what happened to me, I wasn't dealing with all the SHIT that was going on in my life and that shit got stuck in my emotional body and has been fucking with me for years! I believe all the stuff that I had to deal with at a very young age has served me in some cases, but some of the sadness, the worry and the fear got stuck way down and has prevented me from doing what I truly love for a long time. I was so afraid to step out on my own, to get up and speak in front of people, to really share what I had learned about this amazing universe and how it all works. To see myself as a successful life coach, speaker and now an author, really freaked me out, until I started to do the real inner work.

So how do you begin the process of the inner work and how do you know it is working in your life? I believe this happens when you are more aware of your emotions and not so afraid of them. A lot of us are afraid to feel, to really feel the emotions when they come up, so we distract ourselves from them. But I know that not processing your emotions when they arise can restrict us from living life to the fullest unless we learn how to release them.

Sure, I wanted to quit doing the work sometimes. It would be so much easier to try and just "get through" life, but now that my Badass was back, she had a tendency to kick my ass into doing what I needed to do. I would start feeling sorry for myself, thinking of all the shit I had to do, thinking about all the new things I had to learn to build my business, and that is when she would speak up:

"Are you done yet?"

"Are you finished feeling sorry for yourself?"

"Did you forget how powerful and amazing you are?"

"What about all the people that are waiting for you to help them?"

"Time's up, you had your time to feel sorry for yourself, now get your ass off the couch and start moving!"

My Inner Badass can be a bit of a hard ass, but she is right. I take some time occasionally to be tired and feel sorry for myself, but it doesn't last forever anymore. It used to last for days and weeks, now I see myself feeling better in a couple hours. Sometimes I do need rest, and that is OK. If I find myself having a long stretch of stress or frustration and I feel myself going back to "crazy town", I make an appointment with my energy practitioner.

I go to several different energy healers that each have their own way of helping me release my emotional baggage. And that is exactly what it is, emotional baggage. It's like we are carrying around a shit-ton of emotions that we have pushed down because we didn't want to deal with it at the time, but it makes you feel emotionally heavy. It is extra baggage that is not serving you, and once you release it, you start to feel better, you have more energy to do the things you love, and life can actually get better. Trust me, I have lived it.

Whether you believe it or not, we are all made of energy, and when you have trapped emotions, it is like a ball of energy stuck somewhere in your body and it can cause all kinds of issues. It can cause pain, illness, and eventually, in some cases, major diseases. I have actually taken classes on this to understand it more, because at first I thought these people where a little crazy, but I have come to understand it more fully, and now I can help others realize how important it is to do the work on their energy body. That is exactly what Dr. Wendi Jones was doing to me and I believe that it has helped me tremendously through the tougher times in my life.

Another daily practice I do is meditation, it can go anywhere from five minutes to forty minutes, depending on how much time I have. Sometimes I can get into a meditative state by just walking or hiking in the woods. I was walking one day in the park, surrounded by a thousand trees and I just started crying for no reason, and I didn't try to fight it. I just let myself be in the moment and I let it all out and I just loved myself through it. During those times, I feel like I am just processing the emotions that need to come up at the time, and I no longer feel the need to ignore them or push them away.

Here is the thing, we are all operating on about 5% of mind being conscious decisions and 95% of our actions and habits, patterns and feelings are subconscious. Most of us can't remember what we ate two days ago, or how we got to a meeting last week. We are on auto-pilot most days, just operating through old patterns and habits. That is our subconscious mind controlling us and we don't even know it. So most of the time we don't even know why we are doing or saying certain things.

And at other times we don't even know why we are sad, angry, upset, or hateful, because those emotions are sometimes instilled in our subconscious mind. These can even be feelings and beliefs from other people that we have come to take on as our own. That is why it is so important to release them if they don't serve your higher purpose.

So when I was crying like a big old baby in the park, I didn't even know why that was happening, I didn't go there to do that, it just happened. Crazy, right? But I knew enough to know that I was releasing something from my past. It felt like a ton of bricks had left my body. The funny thing is, I had never gone live on Facebook until that day in the park. I was a little afraid to put myself out there. I thought it had to be perfect and professional, but that was obviously slowing me down. I also thought I would have a lot of critics, but I had to let that go and say, Fuck it, I am doing it anyway, and I did. I did the Facebook live and this time, instead of being a distraction, it was a part of my healing. So much better that way!

I believe we are all a work in progress and it never stops. It can be a little overwhelming sometimes, but I believe the payoff is worth it.

How about just sitting with yourself and being? You don't even have to think, just be. Interesting right? Have you ever done it? Can you just be with yourself? (No dirty thoughts please, at least not during this exercise.) We are human *beings*, not human *doings*, we don't have to be *doing* something all the time to prove our worthiness. This is a great practice to learn how to connect with your inner badass, your inner soul. This is where you find the answers you are searching for. Remember, our life is an inside-out job. It's funny how some of us think being still doesn't work for us, but I have come to find out that when I have questions, the answers I usually am looking for come to me later, after just being still for a while, especially when I stay in the practice of being aware of things around me.

So, these are the life skills and tools that I used to keep myself from going back down into the basement, aka that deep dark hole, and I am sharing them with you in case you yourself are stuck in your own hole. But I always believe you know deep down inside what is best for you. Just because certain things work for me, they might not work for you. So simply keep asking yourself if this feeling is adding connection to your Badass Soul? If not, put it aside. And then ask yourself, your God, your universe, what are the tools that would help you move forward in life, so that you can get the results you truly desire?

Just check in with yourself and see if you are playing the distraction game. Are you trying to ignore what is really going on in your life? Are you trying to push scary emotions down deep within so you don't have to deal with them? If you aren't, *great.* But if you are, let the games begin! Feelings are not always fun to deal with, but it can be so much more rewarding than pretending everything is peachy-keen. It can definitely be a roller coaster ride, but it is worth it. The ride is thrilling and scary and exciting all at the same time.

I have lived both ways, and I now understand that dealing with your shit is the best way to live. You might even start to like the person inside of you better. You might see more of your authentic self show up and you could even fall in love with that person. How would that feel? To truly love yourself, what does that really look like? From my personal experience, going from such self-hate that I felt like ending my life, to *Wow, I really love this girl,* told me I am amazing, funny, smart, caring, compassionate, loving, and at the same time. And I can really kick some ass when needed. I know I am not perfect, but I don't have to be in order to love myself, and that has changed everything.

I know I have grown as a person and continue to do so on a regular basis. I am so glad that I tuned into myself and saved my own life, because now I believe I can help others get through their own shit-show. There is another side, a calmer, peaceful, happy, fun side, and people need to know that.

I have been told that people aren't really afraid of failing, that they are more afraid of how powerful they truly are. Interesting: could you imagine if we all got back to our genius state of mind that we were born with? My mentor Mary Morrissey has said that we are all born with a genius mind and by the time we are five years old only twenty one percent of us use our genius mind and by the time we are twenty one only five percent of us use our genius mind! *Wow,* that's how conditioned we get by society and how disconnected we get from our true self. God gave us these genius minds to create whatever we want, and it is never too late to connect to them if we keep getting centered and keep learning.

So, don't be afraid of staying focused on what you truly think you are capable of achieving. Don't distract yourself from the dreams and goals that you truly desire. Reconnect to your Soul's purpose, love yourself through the good times and the bad, and stay strong enough to go kick some ass out in this world. We all have gifts that have been given to us to be utilized, and it doesn't serve anyone if we don't express them out into the world. The world needs what you have to offer.

# CHAPTER 10

*Feels Good To Be Alive*

F ast forward, well not too fast, it seemed like forever to get to a better place in my head and in my heart, but I was glad I did. It felt good to be alive again, I had such a great life and I was tired of dragging my ass through it. I wanted to live full out, I turned 50 in 2016 and I was ready to celebrate my life, I was so happy I remembered who I was and knew I was stronger than the conditions in my life. I was really proud of myself and that didn't happen too often.

So, celebrate I did! And I celebrated by deciding to say yes to everything that sounded fun and exciting to me. I took twelve trips that year, some small, some life changing, but my goal was to have my 50th year be my best one yet. It started out by going to Nashville to go see Madonna in concert with some of my best buddies, and it was a blast. My stomach hurt so much from the laughter that went on the entire weekend. My favorite memories are the ones of the late-night dancing in our hotel rooms and using the bed runner as an accessory and cape. And the talks that went on to three or four in the morning, those are the best of times. And of course, even though she is always at least two hours late, Madonna always throws a good party.

Then I went to the Lake of the Ozarks in February, which is only a couple hours from St. Louis where I live. I went with my very best friends that I travel with all the time. The lake trip for us is a quick getaway for us to shop, eat, drink and laugh our asses off. Sometimes we even spend half a day at the spa, which is my favorite self-care thing to do. We never have to go anywhere special to have a good time, we crack ourselves up and think we are hysterical. (We kind of are.) We have a tag line we use for our friendship: *I love us!* That is always a trip we go on every winter just to make sure we are together to plan our bigger trips for the year ahead.

Then March came around and it was time for my birthday parties. I have the privilege of being born on March 17th, St. Patrick's Day. That year I looked at my life and I intentionally celebrated that I was *alive*! St. Louis has two parades in March, so for the first one, I had all my friends and family get hotel rooms and we spent the day downtown. I was so blessed to have so many people celebrate with me. Then we did it again for the parade in Dogtown, a St. Louis neighborhood, on St. Patrick's Day and my birthday, March 17th. As usual, it was quite a celebration, me in my Irish kilt with all my favorite people around me.

*Michael, Mick, Me, MaryKate, Kristen, Mimi, Casey, Danny, and Julie Doherty*

*Sean, Brian Gary, Me, Shane my Nephew and my brother Mick*

*Deb, Stathy, Theresa, Marge, Yvette, Teresa and Marcia*

*These are mostly all cousins from my father Tom and his twin brother Art*

I was not the only one celebrating a big birthday that year. My oldest daughter Maggie was turning sixteen and my youngest Brooke was turning thirteen, so I planned a trip to Mexico for a week to celebrate everyone's birthday later in March. One of my best friends Debbie and her daughter Allie joined us and we had an amazing trip. I still remember the smell of that place, it was so incredible. I think of that trip often. There were times that I would just sit there on the beach all by myself, tearing up, and having a conversation with my Inner Badass about how glad I was to have her back!

My favorite story from that trip is when we got hustled into going on one of those timeshare tours. We did it, so we could get the free trip to the Jungle Zip Line park for our families. We got free lunch at the Moon Palace, and a little golf cart tour of the whole place, which wasn't too unbearable, but having been on the tours several times at other places we all knew what was coming. Plus they keep giving you drinks to get you relaxed so you'll be more willing to sign on the dotted line at the end. Well, Gary, Debbie and I were not interested, and clearly didn't have the hundred grand they were looking for to buy their timeshare. These things are a whole production: when you say no to the first salesman, they send you to another salesmen, and after saying no to them, they get you a little private room and some more liquor. I mean, this goes on for hours and we were laughing so hard because these people were not giving up.

Finally, we thought it was over and they told us how to exit to the next step to get our free passes for the ziplining, but we were wrong. There was another salesman at the end trying to explain that this would be a good investment and he was drawing some circles and numbers on some paper. I don't really remember what they were. But I do remember Gary taking the paper and he started drawing his own circles about what we could do with our money instead. At this point we had become a spectacle. Debbie and I were laughing so hard we had to squat in order to prevent peeing all over ourselves. The salesman *finally* gave up, and started to crack up himself. Reluctantly he took us to the counter to get our free passes. It was so worth our time, the jungle tour was amazing and our families had a blast, and we got a great story out of it.

By the time April came around I was *done* celebrating my birthday. My fifty-year old body couldn't handle any more. My daughter's birthdays were coming up and I wanted to focus on them. But my husband had other plans. He had asked my brothers to get me out of the house on the first Saturday in April, because he was planning a surprise party. A party that I asked him over and over again not to plan. We had many discussions that I *did not* want a surprise party because we were celebrating at the parades, and I had several trips I wanted to take that year and wanted those to be my presents. I even told my friends to stop him if he said anything to them. They tried, but there was no stopping him.

So two of my brothers invited me to go furniture shopping with them in Washington, Missouri. Their friend's father makes really nice furniture down there and they wanted me tag along with them to check it out. I didn't think nothing of it, we hang out all the time. So I got in the car and the first thing out of my mouth was, "I am so fucking done with my birthday, I am glad it's over with because I am exhausted." They were dying inside because they knew there was a big party waiting for me when I got back home.

So we shopped for a couple of hours and actually bought some furniture. Then we stopped at a place to have lunch and a couple drinks, and by this time I was pretty tired, so we headed home. I was so tired I just wanted to crash when I got home. We were pulling down the street and there were cars everywhere and I said, "Who is having a party? And why wasn't I invited?" That is how clueless I was. Why would I think Gary would listen when I said *no birthday party*! We pulled into the drive way and I got out, still clueless and then I heard them: Doherty voices. My family has loud boisterous voices and I could hear them inside. I turned to my brother Sean, he was grinning from ear to ear, and I said, "Are you fucking kidding me? I *can not* believe you all did this!"

Of course I went in, everyone yelled, "Surprise!" and I looked right at Gary and say, " I am going to kill you!" I also gave my girlfriends a little grief for allowing this and also apologized to them for having to celebrate my birthday for the *third* time. Of course we had a ton of fun and made a lot more memories. That will be a birthday we will talk about forever.

*Walking in for my surprise party*

Then summer came around and we did several Lake of the Ozark trips with family and friends. Then in July we went to our all-time favorite place that we go to every year, South Haven, Michigan. It has a small town feel where the kids are able to roam on their own. We rent a small cottage on the beach and my kids don't want to go anywhere else, they love it.

Then in August I was fortunate to be able to go to Greece to celebrate my good friend Stathy's fiftieth birthday with my other friend Debbie. The three of us have known each other since we were sixteen. I became good friends with Stathy in high school because we cracked each other up, then I met Debbie in a high school parking lot after a football game. She needed a ride home, and we hit it off instantly. It might have been the fact that I had a car and a trunk full of vodka and lemonade. The three of us have been friends for over thirty-five years!

That was why I did not want a birthday party for my fiftieth, because I wanted to go on this trip really badly, and the minute I walked into my house for my surprise party I thought to myself, "Shit, now I can't go to Greece."

But Gary surprised me again and said he talked to Stathy and he let her know that I was going to be able to make it. Needless to say it was a trip of a lifetime. Deb and I got to Athens a day before Stathy so we got to check out the entire city. Stathy still has family there and goes there almost annually, so she skipped that part of the trip. We were so tired that first day, we ordered drinks and scheduled massages. When they asked us if we wanted to go together we said of course, thinking go together at the same time. But when we got there, they called us back at the same time for our "couples" massage in the same room. We were so tired, we just looked at each other, shrugged our shoulders and went to our tables. We were so tired we both just passed out. We still laugh about our first ever couple's massage together.

It was almost surreal being able to travel and see such amazing places, because two years earlier I didn't even think I was worthy of such great experiences, at least not until everyone around me was happy first. It's really crazy to write this two years later and think, *that sounds crazy to say that*. I never want to return to that state of mind again. Anyway, Athens had so much to see, but the major attraction was The Parthenon, the ancient Greek temple. It was so breath-taking and magnificent that we just walked around in awe for hours. Then we walked all over the city, up and down all the small hilly roads that had hundreds of shops and restaurants to stop at. We shopped and ate our way through the city. It was amazing.

Our next stop was Santorini Island, where we got to stay at one of those beautiful white resorts on the edge of the hill. I have to say the Greek people are some of the hardest-working people I have ever met. They carried all our luggage down those winding roads and were always waiting on us hand and foot. They would also serve us these amazing Greek breakfasts every morning so we could sit right outside on our porch area, in the comfort of our pajamas and look out into the amazing view of the ocean. Then we would go down these long stairways to an infinity pool to relax some more, and there they were, ready to cater to our every need. It was a little bit of heaven.

I loved everything about Greece, It was an amazing experience spent with some incredible friends. Once again I did a lot of reflecting on that trip when I would be looking out into the sea. I could not believe how far I had come in two years. I was stronger than I had ever been and I didn't ever want to go backwards. I had turned to my Inner Badass to save my life and I was going to ride her skirt tails and start to live this life on purpose.

*In front of the Parthenon in Athens*

*Deb, Stathy and I on the black sand beach on Santorini Island*

*The view from our beautiful place on Santorini Island*

Then in September of 2016 I went with my friends Tammy, Yvette, Sue, Stathy, Debbie to an amazing spa and resort in Winter Park, Colorado, for Debbie's fiftieth birthday. It was such an outstanding resort with five-star restaurants and a high-end spa. We hiked, went horse-back riding, went to the spa and spend a lot of time in the hot tub. My favorite memory was the time spent around the fire pit right outside our rooms. The view was incredible and once again, time spent with good friends is priceless. I believe the minutes and hours with these amazing friends of mine over the years have actually helped me to heal. I truly believe that. The love and laughter I get from them has been a life-saver, I know I can tell them anything and they will never judge me. I consider myself extremely lucky to have had the time and money to take all these wonderful trips with them.

*Stathy, Myself, Tammy, Sue, Yvette and Debbie*

My year ended with a family trip to Galena, Illinois for New Year's Eve. We love to get away during that time of the year and Galena has the Chestnut Mountain Resort (for skiing) and a quaint little town to shop and eat at. We have made a lot of memories during those trips that my kids still talk about.

*Good family time*

Why am I sharing all of this? To demonstrate how someone like me can go from being so depressed that I no longer want to go on with my life, to having a year filled with joy, peace, happiness and a whole lot of fun. But this only happened after reconnecting to my Inner Badass. She reminded me how to stand up for myself and to be OK with saying *no* to things that no longer ignited my inner soul. She also taught me how to become my own biggest advocate and to fight for my life again. I spent so much time being sad and feeling sorry for myself, because I had forgotten just how strong and smart I really was, and it was my time to really awaken to the true Kelly that I was.

That was a goal of mine: to gift myself as much as I could that year. It was my reward for fighting back those tough thoughts and feelings that almost took me out. It was a long road to recovery and it was something I kept in front of me to keep going, because there were still days that I wanted to give up, a lot of days actually, but I knew if I kept taking small steps it would get easier and easier to wake up and move towards my dreams.

# CHAPTER 11

*Being An Example To My Girls*

I have to say, one of the most important things that has come out of this whole ordeal is being a better example to my own daughters. If I would have stayed in my martyr and people-pleasing mode, what would my girls have learned? Just to do exactly the same thing, right? I had to be the generation to stop the habits and beliefs that were handed down from my own parents, which I am sure were handed down to *them* from *their* parents. I had to show them how to connect to their own Inner Badass so they could go and live a life they would truly love.

I was extremely upset and guilt-ridden that my daughters had seen me in such a depressive state, with such a beaten-down state of mind. That was really hard on me. I wanted to feel better but I couldn't find my way out right away and the thought that they were seeing me fall apart was awful.

Proving to my girls that you can pull yourself out of a deep dark place if you truly connect with your inner power was one of the reasons for pulling myself out of that hole. I had to show them that, yes, life is hard and it sucks sometimes, but you *can* get through those tough times and it *can* get better. There were still plenty of days that I thought I wanted to give up. It was hard to stay positive and keep moving, especially when there were still days that I felt like shit the instant I woke up. But taking those small steps, any step, towards feeling better kept me hopeful. I was tired of being tired. I was tired of feeling depressed. I was ready to be healthy again and live life on purpose. There was a lot of living to do and I wanted to get busy living it.

As other parents know, raising children can be one of the toughest jobs on the planet. I thought the baby thing was hard, but that was a piece of cake compared to trying to raise strong, independent, kind, and loving children. How do you do that? I read a lot of books from a lot of different authors to see what felt good to me, and then I just winged it.

I did come to find out that I do not own my kids, that I am not here to tell them who they are supposed to be or even how they are supposed to live their lives. My only job is to keep them safe and to guide them so they can make their own mistakes, and their own decisions. If they don't make their own choices at a young age, they won't be able to make solid decisions when they get older. Learning to let them go and be the amazing individuals they came here to be is not easy, but it will benefit them in the long run. We all want to catch our children before they fall, but that only makes them weaker. Occasionally, we have to let them fall and see them back into amazing, strong, super-souls that they truly are.

I have so many stories of all the times I got calls from the principals and the teachers from Maggie's school. I would brace myself for what was coming every time I would see the school's number on my phone. And the first thing they would always say was, "Maggie is fine, but…" And then it would come, *Maggie blah blah blah*. Most of the time I would be on the other side of the phone, shaking my head and grinning to myself. That Maggie is something else. We have taught her to be her own biggest advocate and she has no problem standing up for herself.

One time we got called up to school, I think she was in fourth grade, because she had given a boy a bloody nose. (Reminds me of the time I gave a twelve-year-old boy, who was trying to mess with me, a bloody nose with my lunch box.) The mini Badass doesn't fall too far from the tree. Gary and I went up there and they explained that a boy had pinned her down with her face towards the ground, and when she got up she went after him, punched him in the nose, and kicked him in the balls. That's what I had taught her to do in case someone attacked her. I just didn't expect it to be on the playground at school.

They told us that they have no tolerance for any fighting and Maggie will have to have some consequences. Gary and I looked at each other, and he said, "I got this." He got up and said, "OK, who wants to go outside and have me put their face in the dirt and see how they react? Because I am pretty sure you are not going to be OK with it. So you can punish Maggie if you want, but she is not going to be in trouble at home. We teach our daughter to stand up for herself and to not let anyone, at any time, treat her like shit. So if you are good with telling a little girl that she shouldn't fight back when attacked, you go right ahead, but she knows better than most of you adults here in this room."

She got no punishment. And that was the right thing to do.

That was grade school, and then there was middle school. Maggie got in trouble a lot there mainly for sticking up for the underdogs around her. She would get in the middle of most fights to stand up for someone else being bullied, and we were perfectly fine with that. And in high school she only had a few issues with teachers and she was able to handle them herself. We have taught both our girls how to be their own biggest advocate, and when something doesn't feel right, stand up for yourself and for others. They really have this capability within them at all times, we as parents have to give them the space to learn how to use all their inner wisdom. They have their own Inner Badass they need to connect with, we just have to allow them grow into themselves.

Then there is Brooke, she very rarely gets in trouble. I actually have told her that it is OK to get in trouble occasionally. She simply says, "It's not worth all the screaming and yelling that goes on." She is more of a Quiet Badass. She is pretty laid back, until someone really pisses her off, then watch out! I have seen her go after Maggie several times.

I fully believe letting kids figure things out on their own makes them stronger. I try to not get in the middle of most of their friend issues, even though I really, *really* want to! Solving all their problems only disconnects them from their own Inner Badass. They can handle more than we think.

Now I am not saying we shouldn't offer our advice as we see necessary. I talk about everything with my kids, I mean everything. Drugs, sex, alcohol, STDs, finance stuff, dealing with emotions, being kind when it's not so easy, whatever comes up and I feel the need to share what I know, I share it. I try not to preach, I just share what I have learned and then I tell them the decisions and choices in life are theirs, good bad or otherwise. My kids will never be able to come back to me and say, "Mom, why didn't you tell me about that?"

Simply communicate with your kids and watch them expand into the most amazing individuals you could imagine. Let them know you will always be there for them, especially during the tough times, and that you will love them no matter what. It's that simple. They are not here so we can live our lives through them. They are their own little souls that need to explore what life has to offer them and for them to follow what truly lights them up.

I also believe that being a better example to them is beneficial to them. They have seen me fail and fall down may times, but they have also seen me never giving up and now they know they have the capacity to fail and to succeed over and over again and that they will be OK. They have learned that this is what life is all about. Getting in the game, taking chances, and experiencing a life that they truly love.

# CHAPTER 12

*Letting Go Of Resentment*

D on't get scared! It's not that hard, if I can do it, you can do it. I have come to understand that resentment is only hurting *me*, affecting *my* health and I refuse to let anyone have the power over me ever again. I had carried it for so long it felt like second nature to automatically feel that way if someone pissed me off. The biggest resentment I carried was against my husband Gary for all the stuff he had put us through with all the different business adventures. I was so angry, stressed out, anxious, and overwhelmed that it took a toll on my health. So obviously I had to blame Gary.

Yes, Gary did play a part in causing some of the stress, but I also had to hold myself accountable for saying *yes* to everything he wanted to get involved with. Gary did not insist or demand that I agree to all of the craziness, I just thought that was my only option, support my husband and agree with all his decisions. I tended to get caught up in his excitement about taken on new adventures, trying something new, or starting a new chapter. It always sounded amazing. But life doesn't always turn out like you want it to, and I didn't handle it well when we failed. Those failures stressed me out.

So, once I started to own all *my decisions*, things started to change for me. I stopped blaming everyone else and I took ownership for my part. This did not happen overnight. It took time to repattern the negative thoughts that had control over my mindset. I had to stop every time some strange voice in my head said, "Look what Gary did to our family." "I hate Gary for making all those mistakes." "I wish I never married him." "It's all his fault." I could go on, but you get the picture. I had to stop and think of a new automatic thought to replace this negative shit, because I knew it was only hurting *me*. And that is what I did and continue to do now when negative thoughts come into my mind. I try to pause and think empowering thoughts that make me feel better and not feel so much anger, hate, frustration, resentment, and blame, it just isn't worth it anymore.

I don't think people think enough about what they are thinking about and how it can affect their health and their path in life. Whatever we are thinking and feeling is actually energy we are putting into the universe and that is what the universe will send back to us. So, if you really stop to consider what energy you are putting out, you start thinking, *I don't want more of that bullshit coming back to me.* It really can stop and make you think more. Paying attention to where your attention takes you is so important. I invite you to join me in thinking about it!

I have learned over these past few years that I have to protect myself from Gary's excitable nature .He tends to put out a tornado-like energy that can suck me in to go along for the ride. I had to learn how to support and encourage Gary to grow when he needed me, but I had to make sure I took care of my needs first. Now, I feel more comfortable letting him know that I need my space and time to build my business, to clear my head, to center myself and to just settle my energy so I can handle anything that comes at me. I don't think he understood why I needed so much alone time in the beginning, but he gets it now and our relationship has gotten stronger.

Marriage is not easy all the time, it is not automatically "happily ever after", and people need to be more honest about it. I see a lot of people pretend that everything is "fine", that their marriage is better than ever, that they have the perfect children and they never fight. I call bullshit on it every time. Yes, there might be one or two marriages like this in the whole world, and maybe it's their second or third one so they've had a little practice, but most relationships have problems and I choose to talk about them. I believe that talking about my own shit-show at home makes others feel OK about their shit-show. We all have situations we are not happy about, but some people are afraid to expose that their relationships may have challenges because they are embarrassed that their life isn't perfect. News flash: *No one's life is perfect!* And it's OK!

Gary and I decided to embrace our shit-show and get through it together. We communicate better, we respect each other's ideas and compassions, we co-parent better and we laugh our asses off as much as we can. Our perspective has changed on a lot of things and we try and approach everything that comes at us as something we can learn from instead of life trying to take us down.

This is just another thing that our kids have seen and hopefully learned from, that marriage is not always easy or full of joy all the time. Tough challenges can come into the relationship. We can choose to handle them, fight, or just give up. So we are choosing to love each other just the way we are, and yes Gary can still push my buttons, and I am sure I irritate him occasionally, but we consider this normal and entertaining at the same time.

# CHAPTER 13

*Gratitude*

I cannot finish this book without expressing how important it is to find gratitude in your heart every day, no matter how hard your day has been. Gratitude has a higher frequency, a higher energy, and it is on the same frequency as abundance. Since I can see the eyes rolling, let me take a minute to explain what the hell that means.

Everything is energy and everything vibrates at a certain frequency. As physical beings, we vibrate at a higher frequency, rocks and other dense objects vibrate at a lower frequency. Words, thoughts and emotions can also be measured as energy, and everything we feel, say or think is a vibration that is put out into the universe and then in turn the universe sends back to us similar energies and vibrations.

Words and emotions like *hate, never, depressed, unloved, worry, doubt, fearful,* and *can't* are considered low vibrational words. When you are constantly putting out these kinds of lower vibration thoughts, you will continue to receive situations, conditions and people that match this vibration. This can get exhausting because you don't even know that it is going on, you are just getting tired of all the bad shit coming into your life. At the same time, words and emotions like *love, hope, trust, happiness, joy,* and *will* are higher vibrational words. When you put out more of these thoughts, you will get back more of those situations. Hopefully this makes a little sense.

Once you understand that changing your thoughts and words can change your life, you become more aware of what you are saying and thinking.

Changing thoughts you are *aware* of can be a little easier than changing conditioned thoughts that instantly show up, due to the way we were raised. Most of us are so conditioned with beliefs and thoughts that aren't even originally ours, they have just been passed down to us. So I invite you to think about what you are thinking about, to be more aware of your habits, to reflect in the evening about things you might want to change.

When you make this a practice in your life, things will start to change for you. You might even get a little bit more curious about how this whole freaking universe operates. You might even realize you have some creative capacity to change things up if you desire.

And it all starts with gratitude, trust me. Play around with it for a while, see if things start to change for the better. Since gratitude is on the same vibrational frequency as abundance, good things are sure to come out of it. There are many ways to start with a gratitude practice. Some people like to make lists, some people just say it out loud, some people do it at dinner time, some do it while they are driving, or during a prayer or meditation time. I just want you to know it doesn't have to be a lot of work. I do it a couple times a day, and I do it by, simply stopping whatever I am doing, and close my eyes and say *Thank you, Thank you, Thank you,* and I can feel my energy changing. I actually get a shitty grin on my face knowing that I am connected to a source that has my back.

And the source can be anything you believe in, a God, the universe, one love, the source, don't get all caught up in the labeling of it, just know that you are connected to it and communicating gratitude to it is key to success and happiness. And not judging others for their beliefs is key also.

Being grateful for things you desire before they come is also very important. I teach my clients to write this when they are getting a vision for their future.

*I am so happy and grateful that...*
*I make $10,000 a month.*
*I am healthy and energetic.*
*I am in a loving relationship.*

And then expect this or something better to happen in your life. Putting this kind of energy around things you desire will help manifest things a lot quicker. I invite you to try it.

I know I don't know everything, but I do know this. I was in a deep dark hole thinking there was no way out, and I knew that if I didn't change some of my daily practices that were destroying me, to ways of how to actually *live* my life, I was not going to be alive very long. And if I did keep living it would not be a pleasant, joy filled, successful life. So I had to make some changes. I had to get curious about how to do things to help me heal and to help me live a life that I *love*. I read books, I watched videos, I got trained for coaching, I started to work on loving myself and I started being grateful for what I did have. And finally things started to turn around for me, it is a lot of work, but I am worth it. I am worthy of an amazing life, and *You are too!* Start the daily practice of gratitude and see how your life starts to change for the better.

# EPILOGUE

This is my mission in life, to help others realize they are worthy of all good things. That they don't have to just take life as it comes, that they have a creative capacity to create what they truly desire for their lives. That is why I have poured my heart out in these first two books. First I had to learn how to be vulnerable so other people knew they were not alone in this thing called life. And then I had to share how disconnection from that Inner Badass can make life more difficult and frustrating, and then I had to share how to reconnect to your inner power. And now my passion is to share everything that I have learned so that we can all live more peaceful, joy-filled, abundant lives. It is possible!

Thank you so much for reading this book. My heart is truly filled with gratitude for each and every one of you.

# ACKNOWLEDGEMENTS

T his may be a first, but I am going to acknowledge myself. I have thanked and dedicated everyone that has been there for me in my first book. So as I was writing this I didn't want to repeat myself and then it hit me, I should acknowledge myself! I am going to publicly thank myself for finally standing strong in my own excellence. I could have quit many, many times, but I kept fucking going because I knew there was something special inside of me that I needed to share with the world. I finally understood that we are all special spiritual beings having a human experience, and we get to choose if it is an incredible, joyful experience or a victim-like experience. And after forty eight years I finally decided to make the most of this gift of life that is given to all of us. I re-connected to my true authentic power and rediscovered who I truly am. I *am a BADASS:*

**B**rave

**A**uthentic

**D**ynamic

**A**wakened

**S**piritual

**S**uperstar

And my mission in life is to help others rediscover their own Inner **BADASS**

And I do want to thank all my family and friends that have always been there for me. I love you all.

Made in the USA
Monee, IL
10 June 2023

35470032R00059